How
Babies
Are
Made

The contents of this book were prepared
in consultation with the
Sex Information and Education Council of the United States (SIECUS)
and Child Study Association of America,
to whom grateful acknowledgment is made.

How Babies Are Made

by Andrew C. Andry and Steven Schepp

Illustrated by Blake Hampton

TIME-LIFE BOOKS, NEW YORK

This is a story about you. Have you ever thought about how babies grow? Have you ever wondered how you were born? In this book, we will talk about how new plants and animals and human beings are created.

When your life began, you were very, very small—even smaller than a dot made by a pencil.

Many living things in this world,
even you, begin life as a tiny egg.

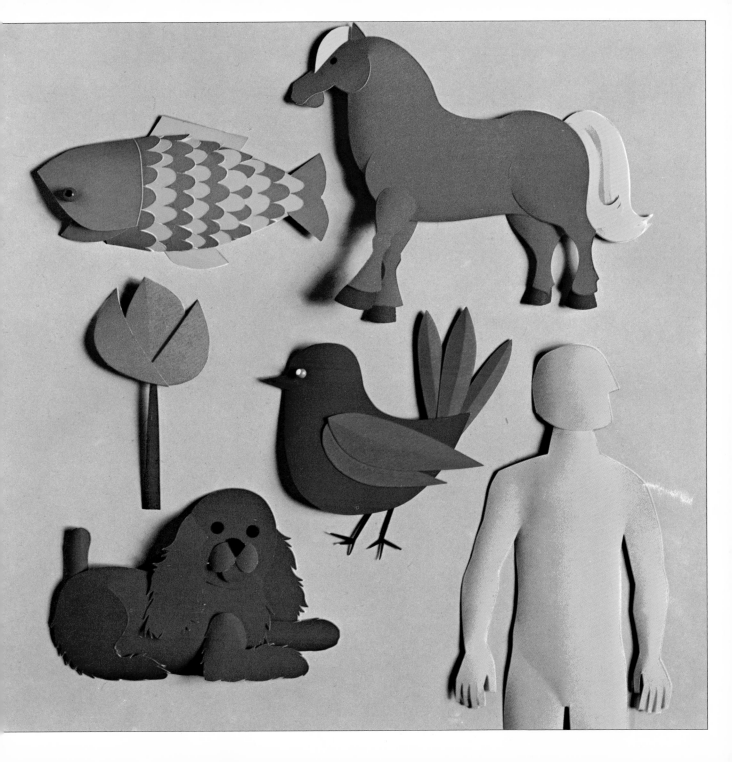

Many plants begin as eggs. Some of these plants have flowers, each of which has eggs hidden within it.

The eggs are in a part called the ovary. In most flowers, the ovary is just above where the petals join the stem.

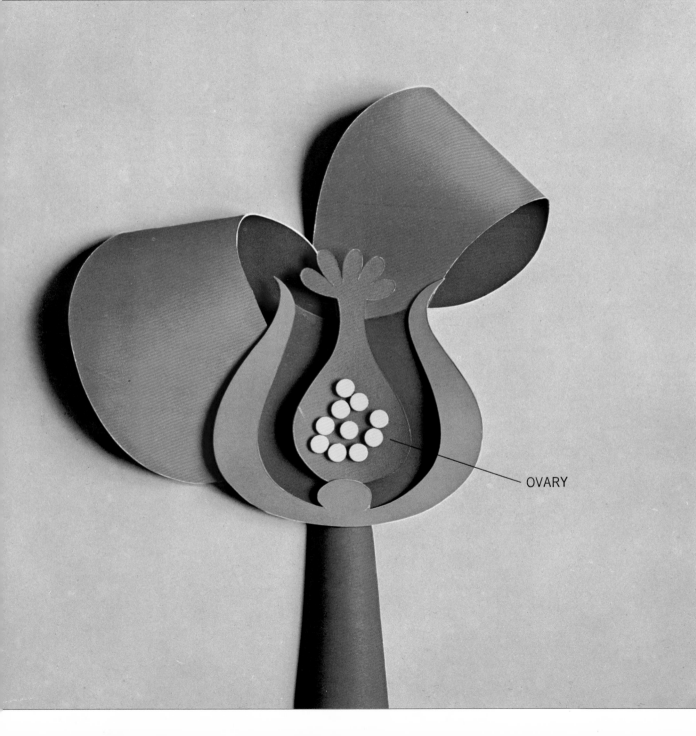

OVARY

The egg cannot grow into a flower seed without a helper. This helper is called pollen. The pollen is often brought from another flower by bees as they fly from flower to flower gathering nectar to make honey. Some of the pollen brushes off the bee onto a part of the flower just above the ovary.

POLLEN

OVARY

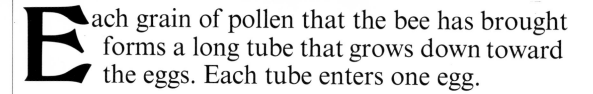

Each grain of pollen that the bee has brought forms a long tube that grows down toward the eggs. Each tube enters one egg.

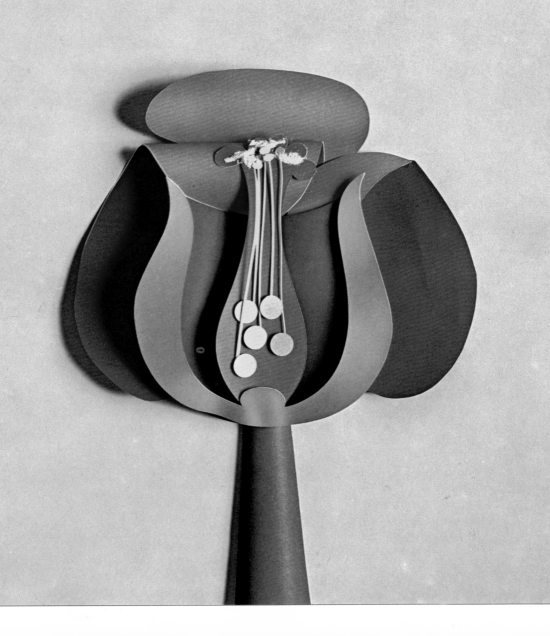

Here is a close look at the pollen tube entering an egg. When this happens, the egg and the pollen join together and change into a seed. This change is called fertilization.

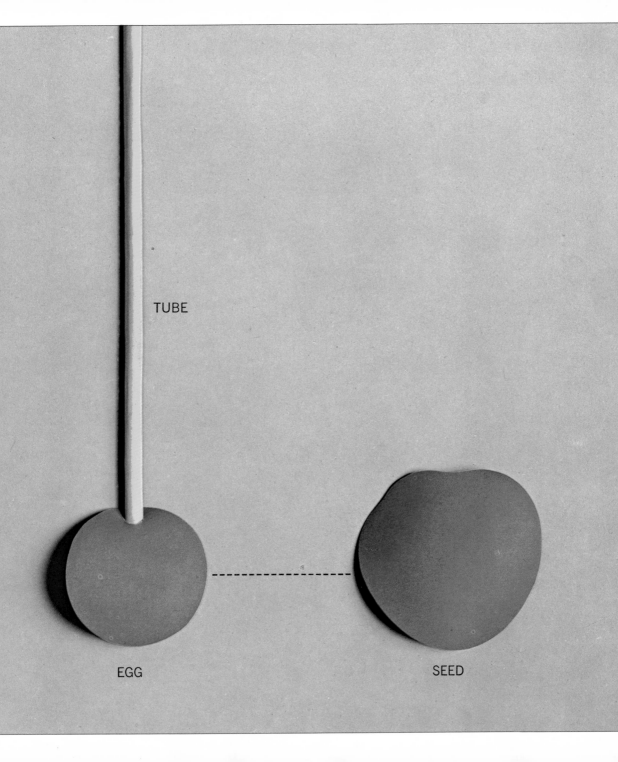

TUBE

EGG

SEED

This seed falls onto the ground. With the help of sun and rain, it will grow into another plant.

So you can see that two things were needed to make this new plant, an egg and pollen.

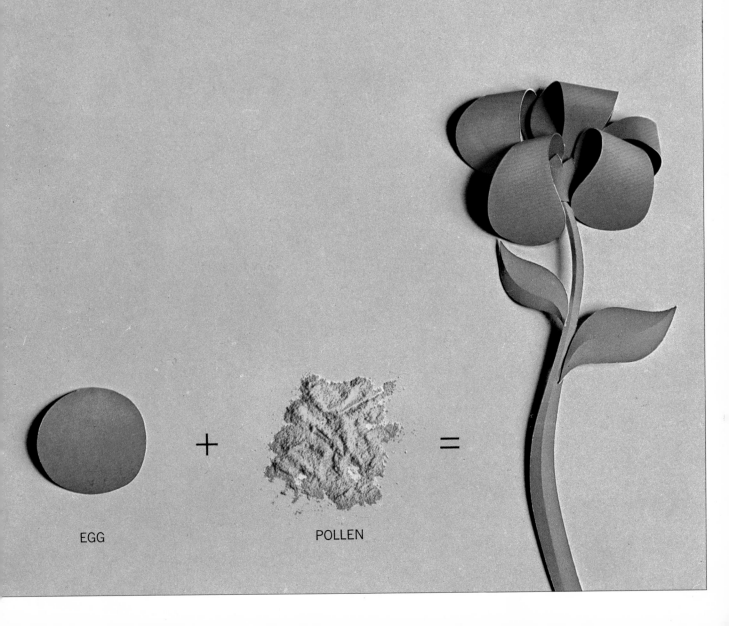

EGG + POLLEN =

Just as it took two things to make this new plant, it also takes two things to make animals like chickens and rabbits and giraffes.

The plant has eggs and pollen. Many animals, like chickens and rabbits, have eggs, but instead of pollen they have sperm. The eggs come from the mothers, and the sperm from the fathers.

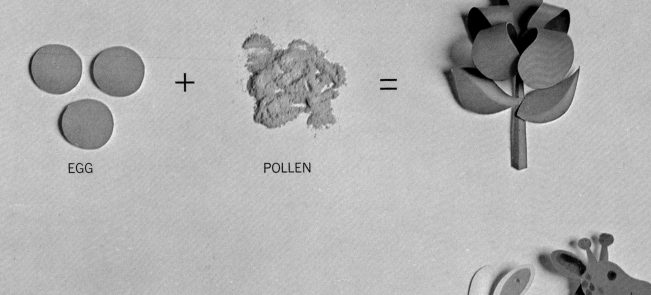

EGG + POLLEN =

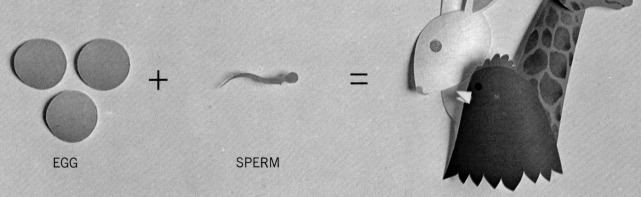

EGG + SPERM =

Mother animals have eggs that are very tiny at the beginning. The father's sperm are even smaller, so small you can see them only with a microscope. Sperm from different animals have different shapes, but they always have heads and tails. The tail moves and helps the sperm swim fast.

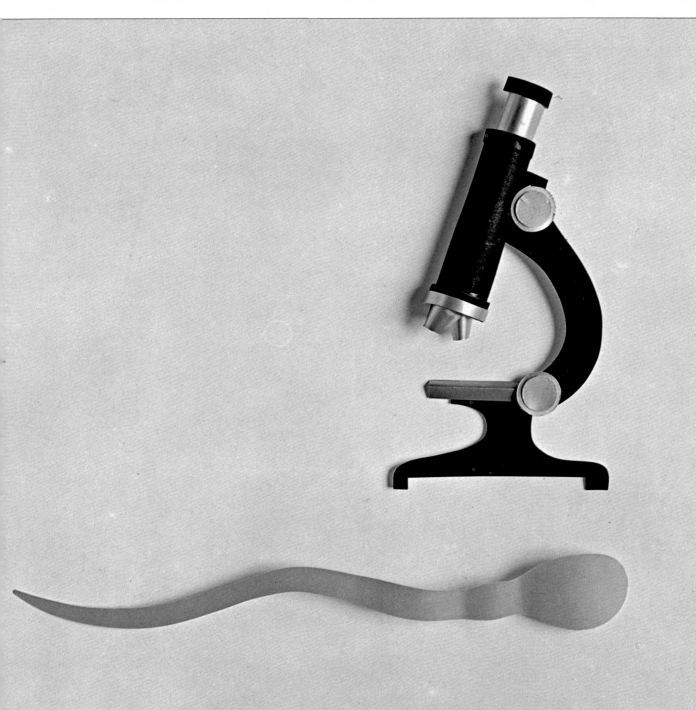

Mother chickens, called hens, have eggs. The fathers, called roosters, have sperm.

The rooster's sperm can join with the hen's egg to make a baby chick.

The hen's egg cannot begin to develop into a baby chick until the rooster's sperm joins with it. To make this happen the hen and the rooster use the openings under their tails.

To send the sperm into the hen's body, the rooster climbs onto her back and places his opening against hers. Then his sperm move into the opening in her body.

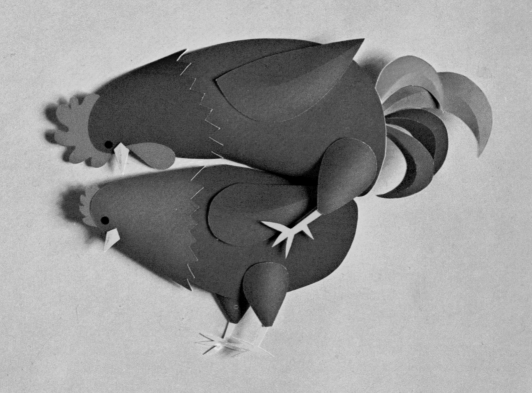

In the hen's body, the sperm swim up from the opening toward the eggs. Some eggs are entered by sperm; some eggs are not. But an egg can be entered by only one sperm. When a sperm enters an egg, a change takes place, the same kind of change as when the pollen joined with the flower egg. And this change is also called fertilization.

As the changed or fertilized egg develops into a baby chick, a shell forms around it to protect it. In one or two days the hen lays the egg in a nest. The egg comes out of the same opening that the sperm went in.

The mother hen sits on the egg in a nest and keeps it warm. After about 21 days . . .

. . . the egg hatches. Out comes a new baby chick.

The hen also lays eggs that have not been fertilized by the rooster's sperm. No chicks will ever grow inside the unfertilized eggs. Usually the eggs we eat are unfertilized.

Eggs

How do puppies begin?

In dogs, as in cats, horses and many other animals, the father's sperm come from parts of his body called testicles. The sperm go out of his body through a special tube between his legs called a penis. Close behind the dog's penis are two little bags that hold the testicles.

PENIS

TESTICLE   TESTICLE

When a father dog wants to place his sperm in a mother dog, he climbs on her back. This is called mating. He places his penis inside an opening in her body called the vagina and then lets his sperm go into her.

The sperm swim up to the eggs, which are in the ovary. In the ovary, an egg is entered by one sperm. Now the egg is fertilized.

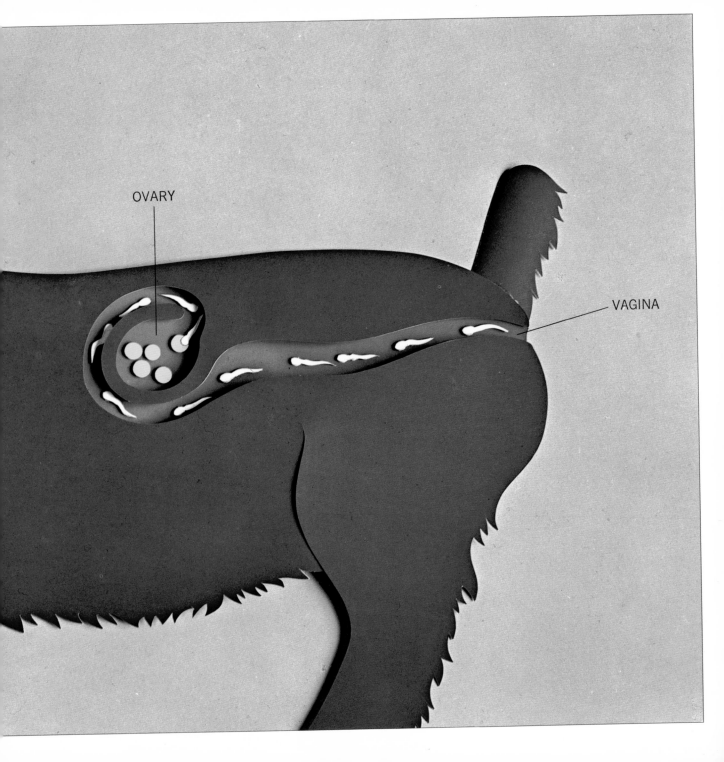

OVARY

VAGINA

After it is fertilized, the egg leaves the ovary and moves to another place, called the uterus. There it begins to grow into a puppy.

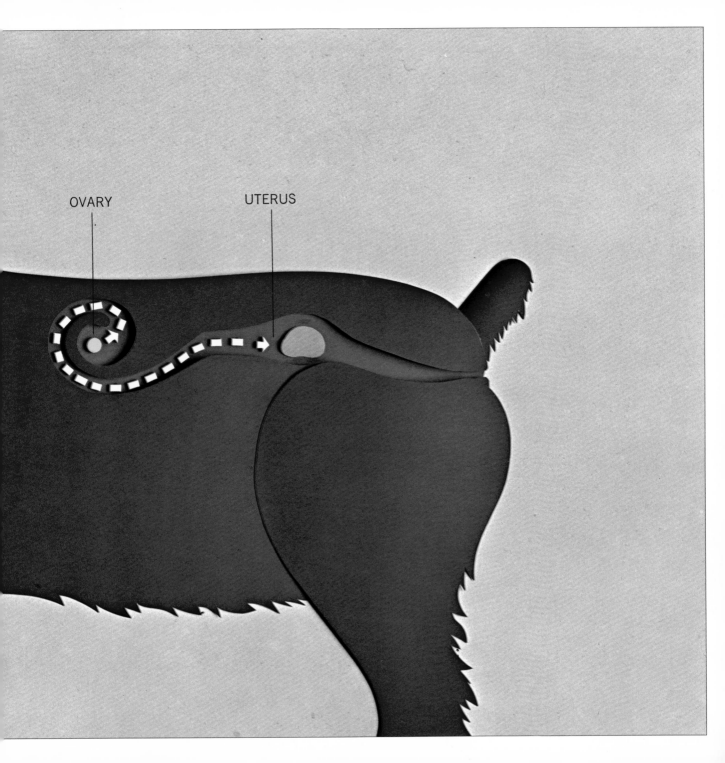

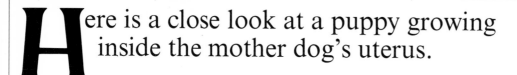

Here is a close look at a puppy growing
inside the mother dog's uterus.

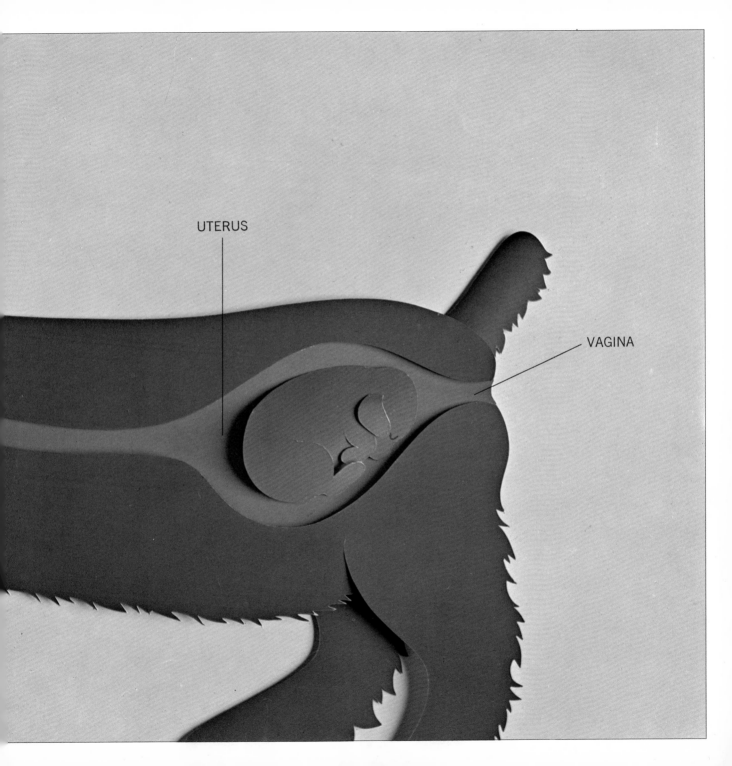

After growing inside the mother dog's uterus for eight or nine weeks, the puppy is ready to be born. It comes out of the mother's body through her vagina. This is the same opening that the father's sperm went into.

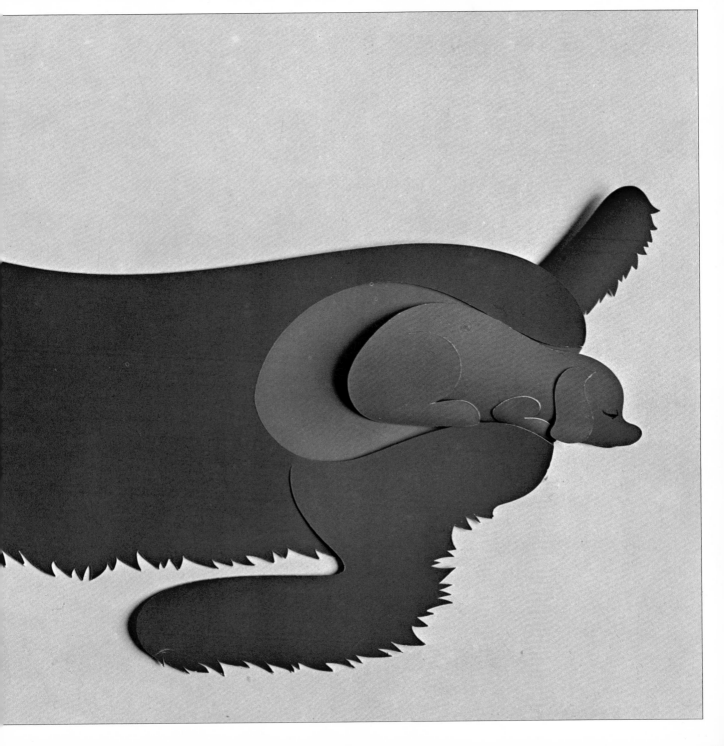

A mother dog can have more than one puppy at one time if more than one of her eggs is fertilized. After the puppies are born, the mother dog lets them drink milk from her body until they are big enough to eat other foods.

Just as mother and father dogs take care of their babies, human mothers and fathers also take good care of their babies and love them very much. How are human babies made?

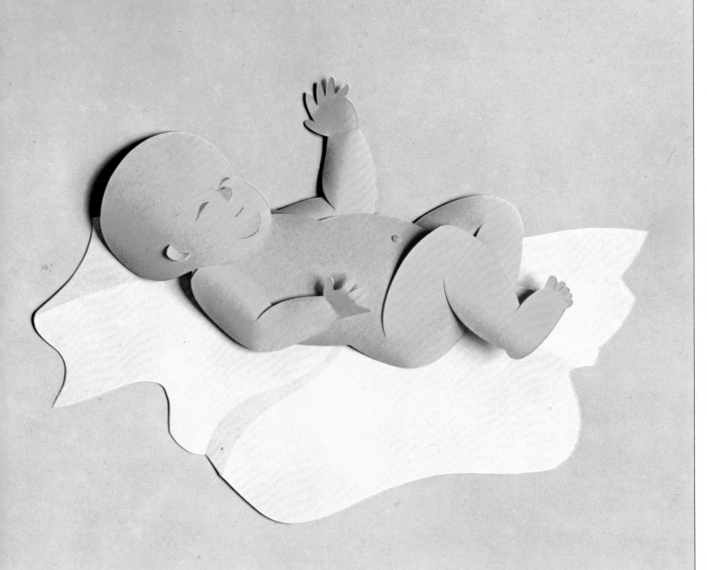

Human babies begin just like chicks and puppies. A sperm from the father must join with an egg from the mother.

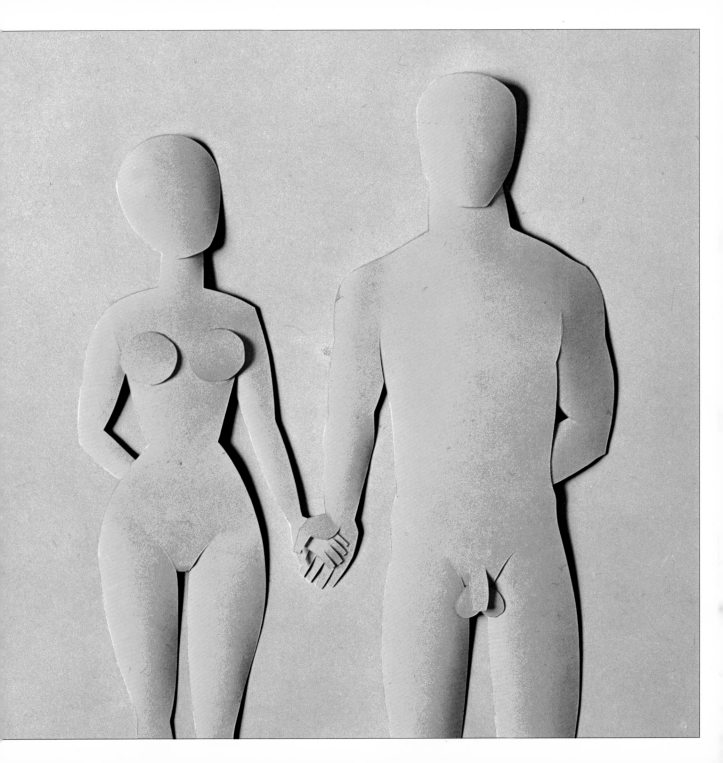

The sperm, which come from the father's testicles, are sent into the mother through his penis. To do this, the father and mother lie down facing each other and the father places his penis in the mother's vagina.
Unlike plants and animals, when human mothers and fathers create a new baby they are sharing a very personal and special relationship.

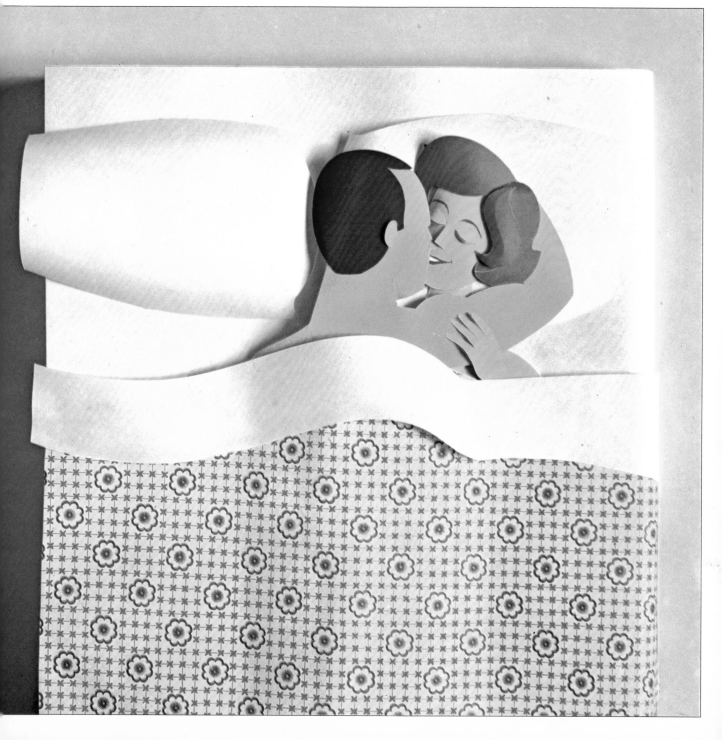

When the egg leaves the mother's ovary, it is ready to be fertilized. The father's sperm swim up toward the egg. Many sperm may meet the egg, but only one sperm will go inside it and fertilize it.

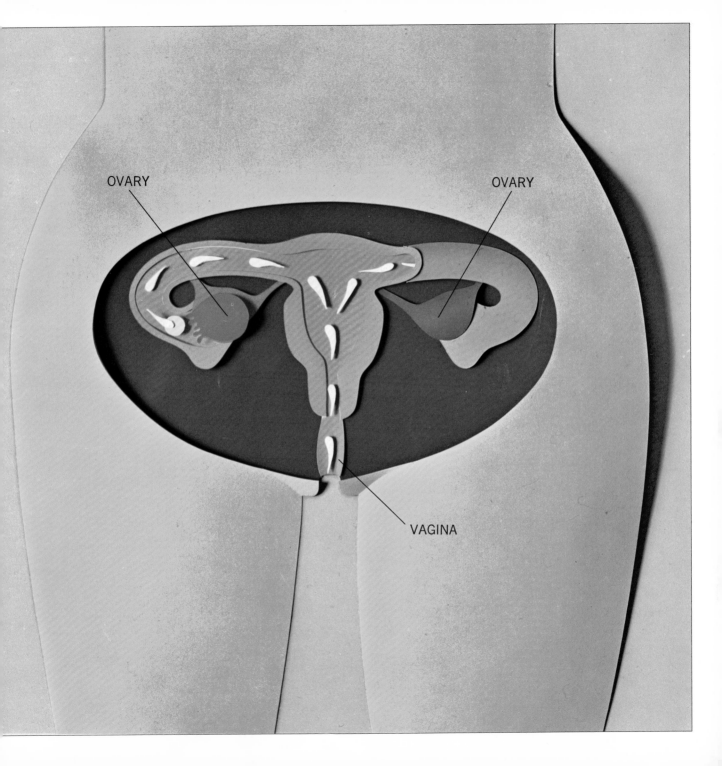

This fertilized egg then moves toward the uterus. The egg will stay here and begin to become a baby. You began just this way. A sperm from your father joined with an egg from your mother. You began to grow while you were in your mother's uterus.

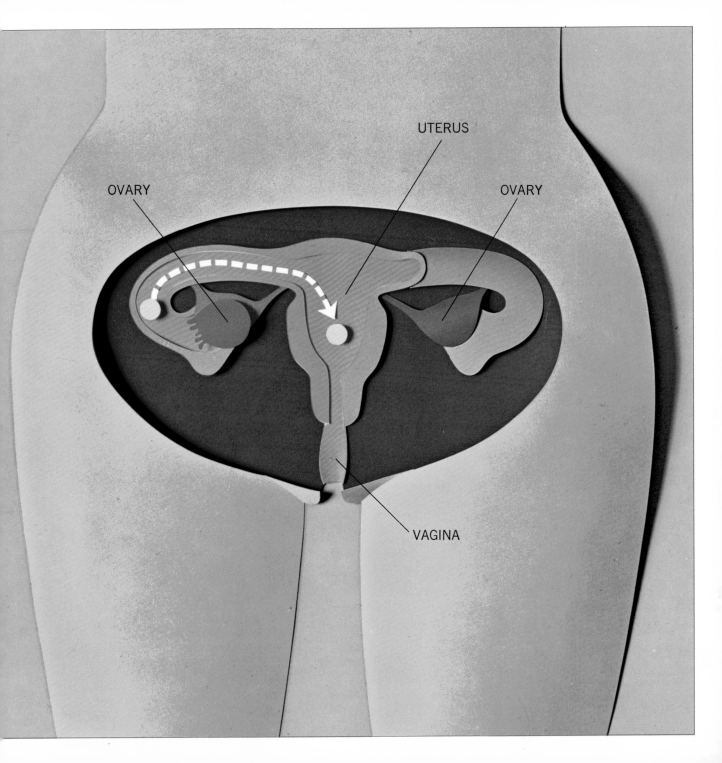

After eight weeks in your mother's body, your arms and your legs began to form. Soon you started to move a little. Your mother's body was attached to yours by a special kind of connection called an umbilical cord. This cord carried food and oxygen to you because you needed these things to live and grow.

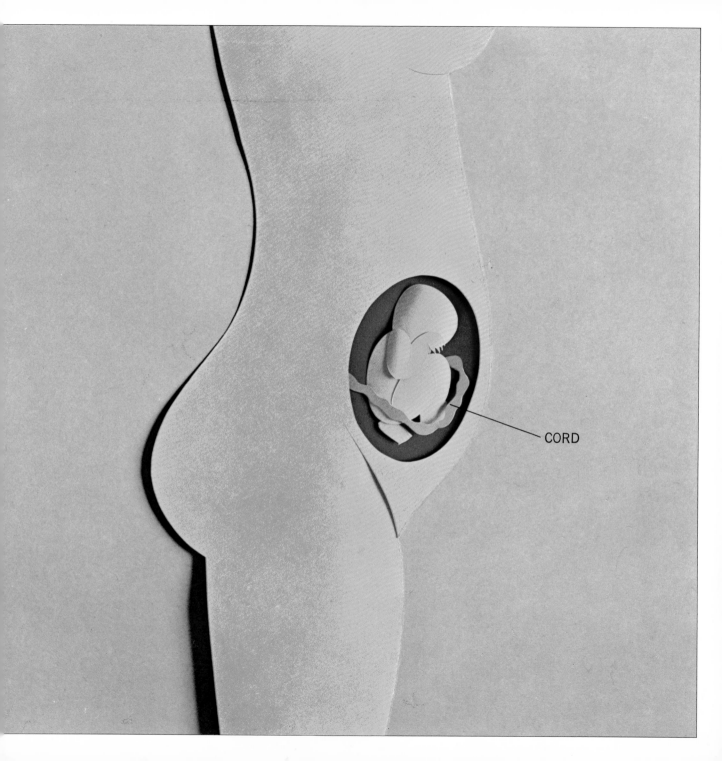

CORD

As you grew in your mother's uterus, the uterus grew larger and so did your mother's body. Then, after nine months, you were ready to be born.

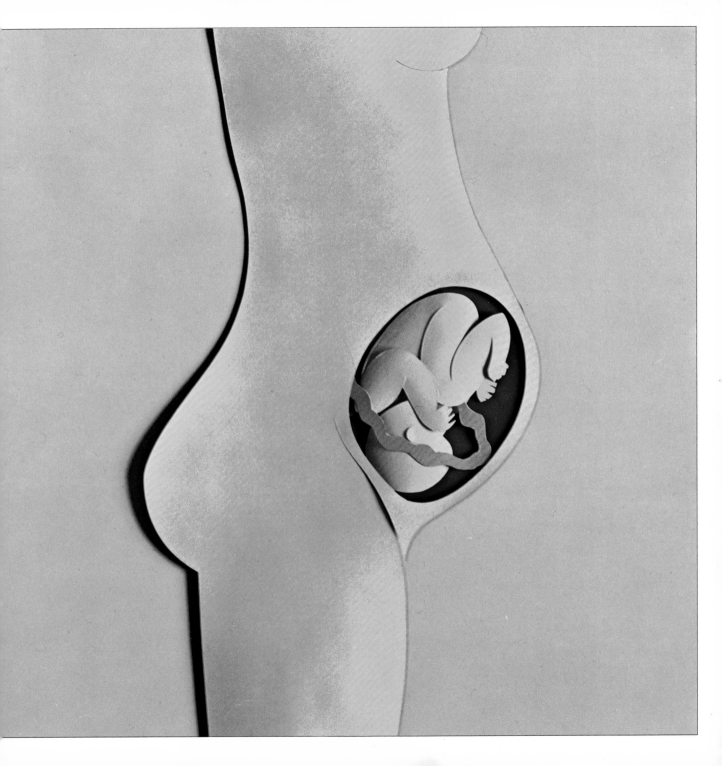

The muscles in your mother's body helped you go out through her vagina. This is the same opening your father's sperm went into when it fertilized the egg. The doctor also helped you out. You were born.

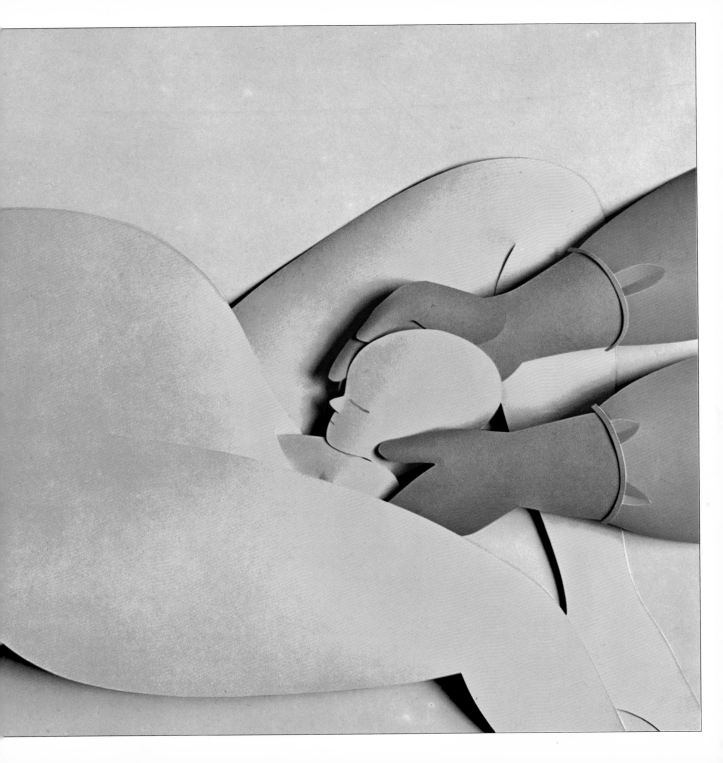

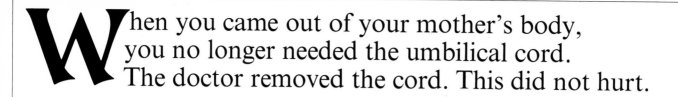

When you came out of your mother's body, you no longer needed the umbilical cord. The doctor removed the cord. This did not hurt.

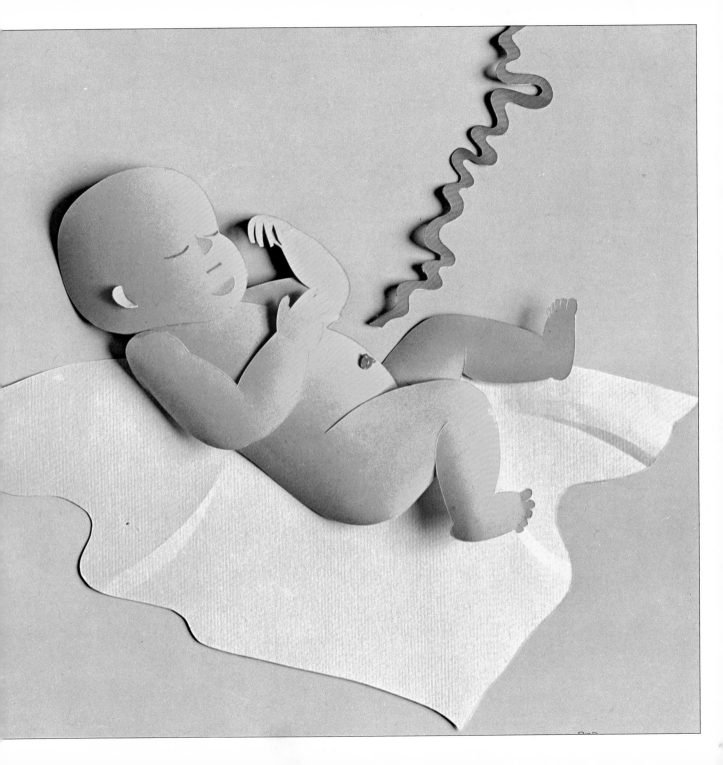

You were born hungry, just like puppies and kittens, and so you had to be fed. You were fed milk from your mother's breasts or from a bottle.

This is how families begin.

And so you were born. That is how your life began. You were not an egg alone from your mother; you were not a sperm alone from your father. You were both, because it was when they joined together that you became alive. All people begin their lives this same way.

Caring for the Earth

Let's Save Energy!

by Sara E. Nelson

Consulting Editor: Gail Saunders-Smith, PhD

Consultant: Kate M. Krebs
Executive Director, National Recycling Coalition, Inc.

Capstone
press

Mankato, Minnesota

Pebble Books are published by Capstone Press,
151 Good Counsel Drive, P.O. Box 669, Mankato, Minnesota 56002.
www.capstonepress.com

1 2 3 4 5 6 11 10 09 08 07 06

Library of Congress Cataloging-in-Publication Data
Nelson, Sara Elizabeth.
 Let's save energy! / by Sara E. Nelson.
 p. cm.—(Pebble Books. Caring for the earth)
 Summary: "Simple text and photographs describe ways for children to save
energy and why it's important to do so"—Provided by publisher.
 Includes bibliographical references and index.
 ISBN-13: 978-0-7368-6321-6 (hardcover)
 ISBN-10: 0-7368-6321-4 (hardcover)
 1. Energy conservation—Juvenile literature. I. Title. II. Series.
TJ163.35.N45 2007
333.79'16—dc22   2006008550

Note to Parents and Teachers

The Caring for the Earth set supports national science standards related to conservation and environmental change. This book describes and illustrates ways children can conserve energy. The images support early readers in understanding the text. The repetition of words and phrases helps early readers learn new words. This book also introduces early readers to subject-specific vocabulary words, which are defined in the Glossary section. Early readers may need assistance to read some words and to use the Table of Contents, Glossary, Read More, Internet Sites, and Index sections of the book.

Table of Contents

What Is Energy?

Energy is power.

Fuel, electricity, and heat are kinds of energy.

Resources

Energy comes
from Earth's resources.
Water behind dams
makes electricity.

People use a lot of energy.
Scientists think we
could run out some day.
Earth could run out
of resources like oil.

Help Save Energy

Jenny saves energy
in her home.
She turns off the lights
when she leaves her room.

Sam grabs juice from the fridge. He closes the door right away to keep the cold air inside.

PHILIPS MAGN

Jenny's video game
uses electricity.
Jenny turns off her game
when she's done.

Billy turns down
the temperature.
Then the furnace
uses less fuel.
Billy wears a sweater
to stay warm.

Sara and her mom save fuel.
They bike to the store instead of driving.

Remember to save energy every day. You can save resources by using less energy.

Glossary

electricity—a source of energy; televisions, video games, and microwaves need electricity to work.

energy—power from fuel, electricity, or other sources that makes machines work; energy also makes heat.

fuel—a kind of energy; natural gas, coal, and gasoline are kinds of fuel.

resource—something valuable or useful to people and places; rocks, trees, water, land, oil, and energy are some of Earth's resources.

scientist—a person who studies and tests nature and the physical world

Read More

Bradley, Kimberly Brubaker. *Energy Makes Things Happen.* Let's-Read-and-Find-Out Science. New York: HarperCollins, 2003.

Stille, Darlene R. *Energy: Heat, Light, and Fuel.* Amazing Science. Minneapolis: Picture Window Books, 2004.

Internet Sites

FactHound offers a safe, fun way to find Internet sites related to this book. All of the sites on FactHound have been researched by our staff.

Here's how:

1. Visit *www.facthound.com*
2. Choose your grade level.
3. Type in this book ID **0736863214** for age-appropriate sites. You may also browse subjects by clicking on letters, or by clicking on pictures and words.
4. Click on the **Fetch It** button.

FactHound will fetch the best sites for you!

Index

Word Count: 136
Grade: 1
Early-Intervention Level: 15

Editorial Credits

Mari Schuh, editor; Juliette Peters, designer; Wanda Winch, photo researcher; Scott Thoms, photo editor

Photo Credits

Capstone Press/Karon Dubke, cover, 12; TJ Thoraldson Digital Photography, 10, 14, 16, 20
Corbis/Warren Morgan, 18
Getty Images Inc./Aurora/Todd Bigelow, 4
Shutterstock/Chris Bence, 8; Jozsef Szasz-Fabian, 1; WizData Inc., 6